Principles of Design

Balance and Unity

THE DESIGN CONCEPT SERIES

Elements of Design
TEXTURE George F. Horn
COLOR AND VALUE Joseph A. Gatto
SPACE Gerald F. Brommer
SHAPE AND FORM Albert W. Porter
LINE Jack Selleck

Principles of Design
BALANCE AND UNITY George F. Horn
CONTRAST Jack Selleck
EMPHASIS Joseph A. Gatto
MOVEMENT AND RHYTHM Gerald F. Brommer
PATTERN Albert W. Porter

Principles of Design

Balance and Unity

George F. Horn
Coordinator of art
Baltimore City Public Schools
Maryland

DAVIS PUBLICATIONS, INC.
Worcester, Massachusetts U.S.A.

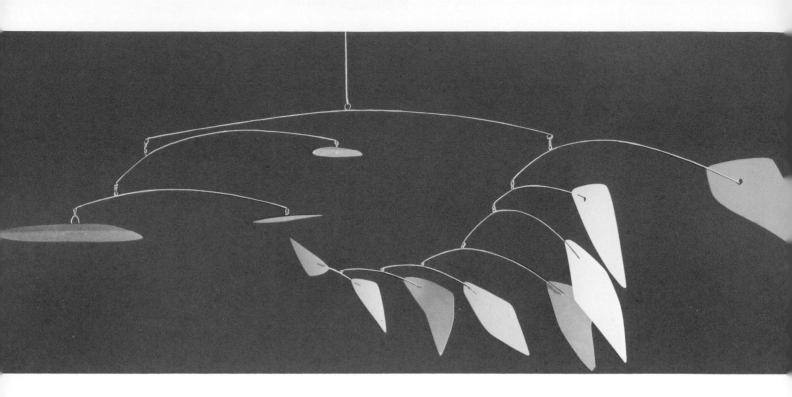

Printed in the United States of America
Library of Congress Card Number: 75-21109
ISBN 0-87192-073-5

Printing: Davis Press, Inc.
Binding: A. Horowitz & Son
Type: Optima Medium
Graphic Design: The Author

Consulting Editors: Gerald F. Brommer,
                     Sarita R. Rainey

10   9   8   7   6   5   4   3   2   1

Contents

Perfect balance is necessary for a perfect ballet performance.

Balance/Unity

Much of the terminology universally associated with the artist, the art critic, the art historian and the art student is not theirs alone. Nor is it a mysterious, separate collection of words that are singular in meaning and useful only in the designing, making or describing of an art object.

Words, such as, contrast, pattern, emphasis, movement, rhythm, balance and unity are recognized, understood and used by most people in their everyday lives. These words are generally accepted along with hundreds of other descriptive symbols that are an integral part of daily communication — spoken, written and read.

Consider the last two words in the series above, **balance** and **unity** (what this book is all about). News items and editorials regularly appearing in papers and journals frequently comment on or describe events, conditions and world affairs that require the use of these two words. We read about *"balancing* the budget", the *"balance* of power", a *"balanced* diet". Important to the production and economy of importing and exporting nations is the *"balance* of trade". The farmer annually deals with *balance* in relation to his crops. A form of the word *unity* is incorporated into the name of the world's most widely known international forum — the *United* Nations. And, of course, the *United* States by its very name continues to generate a sense of *unity* among its fifty states and diverse population.

How often during the past week have you heard or used the words **balance** and **unity** in conversations at home or in school? Or have seen them in your local newspaper, social studies text or science laboratory manual? Think about this the next time you pick up some item to read.

A Sunday afternoon ride on a bicycle built for two requires double balance and a sense of unity.

High in the saddle and balanced to bring home the winner.

Balance in the arrangement of passengers and cargo in relation to the center of gravity of a jet is significant to safety in flight.

A picture of balance, the quarterback stands poised as he quickly selects his receiver. His teammates perform as a unit in blocking the opposition.

Although many words, such as balance and unity, have broad, general application, there are times when they acquire special meaning for specific purposes. This book will ask you to focus on balance and unity in a more limited way. Through illustration and comment it will direct your attention to balance and unity as they exist in our natural and man-made world; balance and unity as they appear in and contribute to the structure and beauty of natural objects; balance and unity as qualities, reflected in the work of the artist, designer, architect and craftsman. In this context, then, how would you define balance? What does unity of design mean?

Suspended in a split-second of time as they leap for a rebound, these two athletes maintain a balance that can only come about through regular practice. They also have a unity of purpose.

Standing on the rooftop like sentinels, this pattern of air vents exhibits a kind of formal balance.

From the air, the cloverleaf pattern of access and exit ramps to the criss-crossed expressways takes the form of formal balance.

Consider first, balance. As you read the next several lines, recall some of your own experiences where the quality of balance appeared as a factor, even though you may not have been aware of it at the time: a painting on display in your school or the local museum; an abstract, steel sculpture in the plaza of a new office building; a flower in full bloom; a manhole cover in the street; your reflection as you stood straight in front of a full-length mirror or a large, shiny plate glass store window. In each of these situations, balance was present.

As you return to these or similar life experiences and continue your close examination of countless things around you, you may conclude that balance cannot be defined as a quality of design with a single characteristic; that there are different kinds of balance. You are right!

Basically, there are three categories of visual balance, into which all things, natural and man-made, may be grouped: formal balance, informal balance, radial balance.

This sturdy oak with its branches radiating outward typifies the stability of formal balance. Note the feeling of unity exhibited by the coordination of branches and trunk.

Balanced on spindly legs, this scavenger of the sea shows little concern for the photographer.

11

These three examples of student art reflect a sense of balance in design and, at the same time, capture the feeling of balance in the three sports represented. The group of stylized figures have been arranged in a pattern that is almost formal in balance. The two single figures illustrate informal balance in design. Note, also, in the group design how the student has achieved unity in his work by bringing the figures close together and through overlapping.

Ptolemy (1953), bronze by Jean Arp. Collection, Mr. and Mrs. William Mazer, New York. Dada, Surrealism and their Heritage Exhibition, the Museum of Modern Art, New York, March 27-June 9, 1968.

From the stern of the oldest floating naval ship, hull and superstructure create a pattern of formal balance.

Formal Balance

Formal balance, sometimes referred to as *symmetrical* balance, projects a feeling of conventional security, uniformity. Objects whose general structure and form are based on this type of balance have a kind of solid, composed, static, even self-satisfied quality. When you are standing straight and are, indeed, an example of formal balance, you have a feeling of stability. If something should occur to cause your body to fall one way or the other (out of balance), you suddenly lose your equilibrium and take immediate measures to return to a state of steadiness and balance.

Have you ever watched two youngsters on a see-saw, enjoying themselves as they moved alternately up and down in a steady rhythm? Have you stood before a formal garden? A decorative fountain, its shimmering spouts of water forming changing patterns in the air above? Or have you looked up at a towering church steeple? Or stared longingly at a shiny, new car from a point directly in front of its chrome-plated grill? As you analyze each of the examples, you will note that they all have something in common: design based on formal balance.

Assuming that the youngsters on the see-saw are approximately the same weight, they will be seated equidistantly from the center of the see-saw. Therefore, what you see to the left of the center will be essentially the same as what you see to the right. In each of the other illustrations, if you place an imaginary vertical line at the center, each side of the now split scene will be identical. These are illustrations of formal balance.

The next time you visit the museum or an outdoor exhibit, see how many paintings, sculptures or other art objects reflect formal balance. Also, look at the natural things around you and the man-made structures in your community that may be considered examples of **formal balance.**

Although this old building is subject to the wreckers ball, its dignified, formally-balanced main entrance poses quietly for one last photograph.

A sparkling fountain in Hopkins Plaza (Baltimore, Md.) is timed to change through a series of formal balance designs.

A uniformity in belief and a security in faith are underwritten in the rugged formality of this church tower.

The arrangement of windows and ornamentation provide a sense of stability to this formally balanced building facade.

Would you consider this a pattern of formal balance?

The crowd is gone and these rows of seats form a stark pattern of formal balance.

A garden, a snow-covered car and a building under construction,
each with its own kind of symmetry — formal balance.

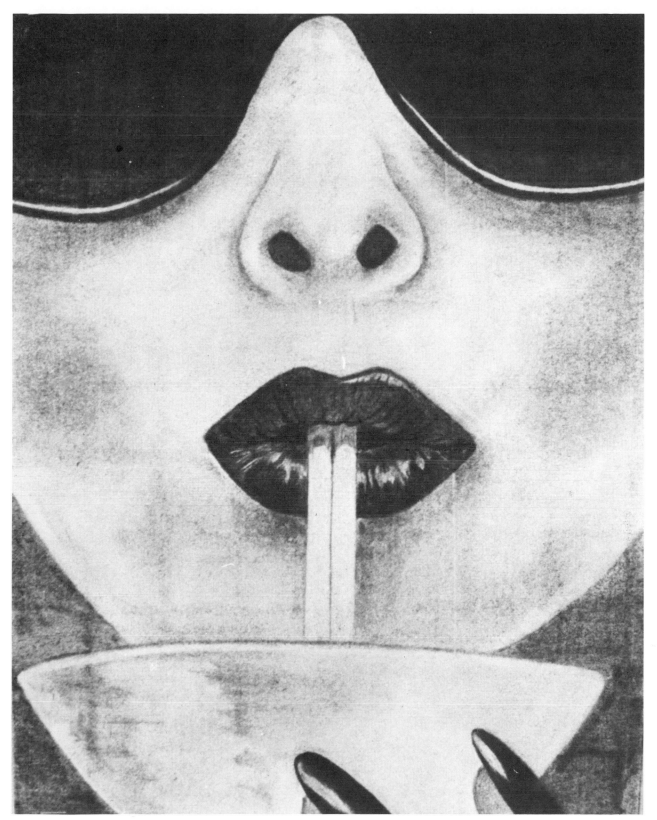

An example of formal balance, this painting by a student speaks for itself.

In each of these studies of natural
form, you should be able to see the
quality of formal balance.

Photograph by Al Porter.

Towers are usually good examples of formal balance. You probably would agree that this is logical since towers extend upward, perpendicular to the surface of the earth. Therefore, they require the kind of design and construction that will provide stability, and a sense of security. Think of the Leaning Tower of Pisa (Italy) and the concern it has been causing for many years. It is gradually moving farther out of balance to eventual collapse, unless something can be done to correct its perilous position.

On the next few pages, there are many different examples of towers. A couple of these, you may not have thought of as being towers (fountain, street light). Yet they do reach up and have the characteristics of a tower.

As you look at these, do they help you to understand more thoroughly the concept of formal balance? Would you say that each of these examples is symmetrical? How many towers can you locate in your town?

Church towers often contain bells. The combination of the ringing bells and the upward thrust of the design serve to point the eyes of the observers heavenward.

Airport control towers are the centers of operations for all aircraft within their control zone.

This water tower is necessary to maintain a steady pressure of water for a suburban community.

The Shot Tower, Baltimore, Md., once used to manufacture cannon balls for Revolutionary War forces, is now an historic landmark.

A late nineteenth-century, early twentieth-century fountain that not only brought beauty to a bristling marketplace, but also served as a water spa for dray horses.

The towering roof of a railroad roundhouse, converted to a museum (Baltimore and Ohio Railroad Museum, Maryland).

This contemporary street light is a tower-form that functions well as it casts its light from above.

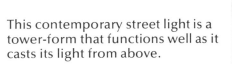

Photographed from a different angle, the Constellation now is an example of informal balance.

At the top of the pole, the wires and crossbars form a pattern of informal balance against the clear, sunny sky.

Informal Balance

Another term for **informal balance** is *asymmetrical* balance. This kind of balance is characterized by its spirited, active quality and by the visual tension that it creates. It often seems that a painting or sculpture based on informal balance is visually out of balance. However, this would really not be true. You will understand this after you become more aware of the characteristics and nature of informal balance.

These familiar symbols of new construction etch interesting and breathtaking linear patterns of informal balance in the sky. Even though the extended, steel arms of the cranes swing precariously about in performing their work, we are assured that the counter-balance, located closer to the central vertical axis will prevent disaster.

In a visual sense, then, informal balance is nonconventional, provocative and forceful. It is irregular and moving, even dynamic.

Picture yourself running. Better yet, when the school day is over, ask a friend of yours to take a fast turn around the track. Notice that as he is running, his body is leaning forward at an angle. However, his leg movement and forward thrust combine to keep him from falling. He is an example of informal balance — moving, active, dynamic.

Returning to the two persons on the see-saw as another illustration, suppose this time one weighs one-hundred and twenty pounds and the other, eighty pounds. In order for them to operate the see-saw to their mutual satisfaction, what do they have to consider? Of course — the heavier person will have to sit closer to the center while the eighty-pounder sits back at the very end of the see-saw. This arrangement is necessary to bring about balance appropriate for a steady up-and-down movement. This is an example of informal balance.

Think of other examples of informal balance in your daily life: the colorful design on your cereal package, an ad in the newspaper, an illustration in a magazine. "Draw" an imaginary line down the center of each. If one side is quite different in appearance than the other, you are looking at arrangements that are informally balanced. Many of the older school buildings are formally balanced with the main entrance located directly in the center of the front facade. However, new school buildings often are designed with a feeling of informal balance. Check your school building and see which it is.

Are you ready now to look at and analyze a painting, a linoleum block print, a piece of sculpture or a ceramic container and determine whether they are formal or informal balance? Try it! Keep looking! See how many examples of **informal balance** you can find in natural objects and other interesting things around you.

The interior wall of a partially razed building (opposite page), piers on a wind-swept beach and a lonely boathouse. Each of these photographic "shots" is an example of informal balance. The heavier shadow on the building wall is located near the vertical central axis of the photograph, balanced by a lighter shadow farther to the right of the center. Do you get a similar feeling with the piers on the beach and the boathouse?

33

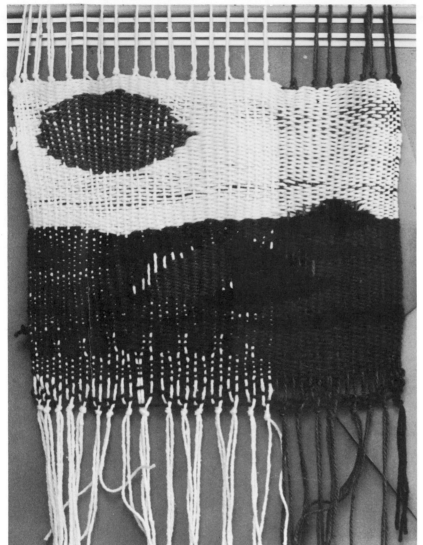

Three works of art in which a feeling of informal balance prevails. The wire sculpture is by a student, Lutheran High School, Los Angeles, California; the weaving, by a Baltimore City high school student. The characteristic combination of free-flowing form and open voids is a sculpture by Henry Moore, located on the plaza of the U.S.F. and G. Building, Baltimore, Md.

Runways and taxi-ways create geometric shapes at Dulles Airport, Virginia.

The photographs on these and the following two pages show examples of informal balance from another perspective. Each of these aerial photographs is a visual record of the interrelationship of man and his environment, showing how man has made an impact on his natural surroundings for various purposes, including survival, recreation, transportation and preservation.

Study the contrasting patterns of informal balance as presented by the various scenes.

The natural informal beauty of clouds and a sunlit bay.

This complex of throughways and curvilinear access ramps is quite informal in the design it creates.

A wildlife preserve with the informal linear pattern of a lonely road.

A huge quarry, carved into the earth's surface. What type of balance does this represent?

Sailing with the wind on Chesapeake Bay, Maryland.

A crowded arrangement of mobile homes, balanced by a curving access highway
to the right.

The seasons of the year alter the appearance of the earth. In the snow-covered farm scene, the cluster of buildings and trees on the right are balanced by the angular roadway, fences and trees on the left. The summer farm scene is still another example of informal balance with a different pattern of lines and shapes.

Morning Star, 1943 Stabile, Alexander Calder. Sheet steel, steel wire and wood painted, 76¾'' x 48⅜'' x 45¾''. Collection, The Museum of Modern Art, New York. Gift of the artist.

This lavishly decorated wheel on an ancient circus wagon gives the appearance of a sunburst.

Radial Balance

Perhaps the simplest type of balance to understand is **radial balance.** The word radial is self-descriptive and can be thought of as radiating from a central point. A universal example of radial balance would be the bicycle wheel which has a central axle and spokes radiating out to a perfectly round rim and tire.

Designs based on radial balance relate somewhat to formal balance in that they are generally static, orderly, quiet and create a feeling of stability and security. The principal difference is that the various elements contained in this type of design are arranged in a radiating sequence around a central point, forming a circular pattern.

One of the most famous architectural examples of radial balance is the Rose window in the Cathedral at Chartres, France. Similar designs, of lesser fame and quality, yet of importance to the particular building, may be seen in church and cathedral architecture in many cities of our country. There may be one in your town. Check it out.

A feature that has appeared frequently in the work of the artist throughout history is the sun symbol. This, too, in its diversity of interpretations, is representative of radial balance.

What common, ordinary natural objects can you think of whose structure or formation is based on radial balance? The next time you slice an orange in half study the arrangement of its segments. Would this natural design be an example of radial balance? See how many illustrations of radial balance you can find in your community. Look for other examples of radial balance in fabric designs, jewelry and surface decoration of ceramic pottery.

A typical application of radial balance in the design of an ordinary church window.

The concept of radial balance may be seen in the structure of many natural things. The illustrations on these pages include the plant formation itself, flowers and blossoms, as well as fruit which has been sliced in half to reveal the interior arrangement. How many other examples of radial balance in plant life can you discover?

Some of the most common examples of radial balance are the designs on manhole covers.

The rugged rear wheel of a farm tractor.

Not a radial tire but the grooves in the tread radiate from an imaginary central point.

Not all roads lead to Rome, but in many small towns they radiate from a central point.

The repeated shape of this oil refinery's storage tanks presents a pattern that projects a feeling of unity.

New buildings that relate are linked together by open space and a unity of design.

The unity of these farm buildings is emphasized by the surrounding plowed land.

Unity

Understanding this quality of design may best begin with reference to unity as it affects your school experience. Traditionally, educational institutions — administrators, teachers and students — have exerted considerable effort to generate a sense of unity within the school. This is necessary for smooth daily operation, if the students are to accomplish the goals of their educational, social and extra-curricular activities.

Make a study of your school to determine how the spirit of unity exists as an important element: a single school symbol used on banners, book jackets, sweaters and yearbooks; a unity of purpose and interest in the development of curriculum programs, club activities and social functions; the significance of unity for the various athletic teams to perform as teams. You can probably think of many more instances where unity prevails within your school.

What does **unity** mean, then? Would words, such as, "singleness," "oneness," and "completeness" be descriptive of unity? How does this relate to the visual appearance of our natural and man-made environment? To the product of the artist and designer?

Here again, your attention is directed to the physical environment in which you live. Look at individual things such as a tree, a flower, a street light, a poster on the side of a bus or a building. Each of these is comprised of various parts. Do they seem to fit together as single units? Why?

Now look at a larger segment of your community scene; a segment that consists of several parts, such as, a shopping center; an urban renewal area made up of buildings, green areas, fountains, exterior art; a garden. Do you feel that the separate parts (buildings, for example) relate well to each other? Are they integrated into a unified whole?

On your next trip to the museum or to an outdoor art exhibit, look carefully at a painting, a print or a piece of sculpture that you especially like to see how the artist has arranged the individual parts of his design to achieve a feeling of **unity**.

Do you have a sense of oneness in this photograph of a tree, its gently curving branches covered with snow? Why?

Detail of a cast aluminum relief by Jordi Bonet, Canadian artist. Flowing
lines, combined with varying textures, result in an interesting unified
pattern.

The opposite of unity is disunity. Although there are many examples of beauty in our natural and man-made environment, man has often been quite careless and often neglectful or unconcerned about the appearance of his world. Since visually distracting features in our environment are so widespread, examples are included here to emphasize the need to take action to eliminate this kind of pollution from our surroundings. Study the photographs on these pages. Do you like what you see? Are there similar scenes of disunity in your community? What do you think can be done to remove visual eyesores such as these from our environment?

A discarded tire, rubble and junk on a vacant lot.

Clutter along an interstate highway creates a visually discomforting scene.

A sign of carelessness, a note of visual discord.

Obviously no attempt was made to establish a sense of unity between the elements in this photograph.

Momentary disunity, necessary to the demolition of these deteriorating buildings. Will this be replaced with a symbol of unity?

Two good examples of unity of design in this student art.
Note how the animal forms in the print are unified by
overlapping.

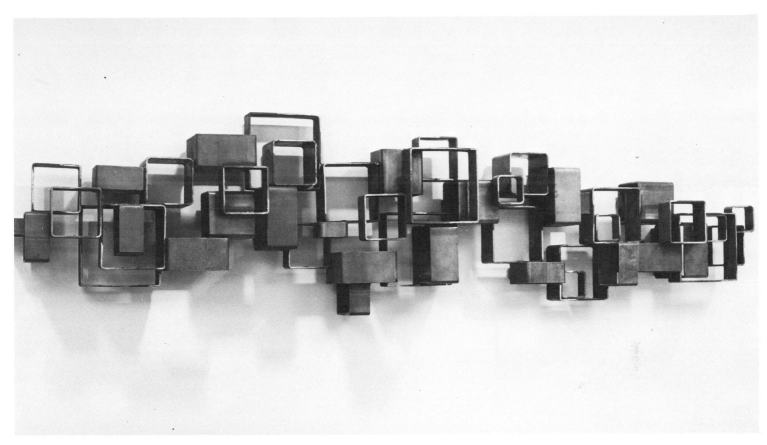

Sculpture by Janet B. Browne, located on the wall of the Waverly branch of the Maryland National Bank, Baltimore, Md. The many units in the design are unified by overlapping.

Hexagons of Douglas Fir from British Columbia, arranged in diminishing sizes as they rise upwards, from the roof of the "Man in the Community" theme pavilion at Expo 67, Montreal. The apertures between the beams, the largest beam weighing 80 tons, were covered by translucent canvas.

Balance and Unity: the artist/designer

The history of mankind is mirrored in the work of the artist. The political, religious and sociological concerns of diverse societies are reflected and recorded in paintings that may range from the relatively small in size to expansive murals and frescoes. In a similar way, the three-dimensional work of the sculptor, often monumental in size, speaks to us of the customs, interests, activities and distinguishing characteristics of cultures of the past and present. The architectural giants of yesteryear stand in testimony to their creators in much the same way that large urban complexes and new cities echo the tone of the twentieth century. Crafts, products of industry and symbols of visual communications all have a role in history in addition to being significantly influential forces in our lives today.

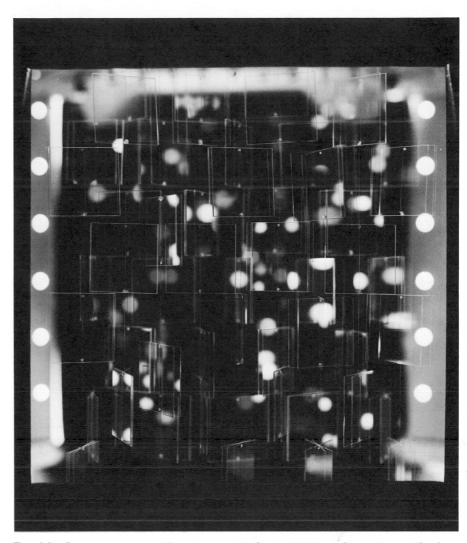

Double Concurrence — Continuous Light, 2 (1961), Julio LeParc. Black wooden Box, 21″ x 19¾″ x 5⅝″ with illuminated aperture 7⅞″ x 8″ in which 54 plastic squares, 1½″ x 1½″ are suspended from 18 nylon threads; mirror backing 11⅞″ x 16″, 2 reflectors, 3 sets of interchangeable pierced metal screens, 2 glass filters. Collection, the Museum of Modern Art, New York, Philip C. Johnson Fund.

Poro Society Mask, wood, fibre, fur; 18″ high.
Sculpture, African, N'Gere, Ivory Coast Collection, The Baltimore Museum of Art, Baltimore,
Maryland; gift of Mr. and Mrs. Leonard
Whitehouse and Dr. and Mrs. Bernard Berk.

60

The artists, architects, designers and craftspersons of past centuries, in a similar manner as those of today, worked with many different kinds of materials and tools to give visual shape to their ideas. They used a variety of techniques and processes — and still do. They were and are challenged by the form and function of their product.

A huge bubble dome, 187 feet high and 250 feet across, enclosed the United States Pavilion, Expo 67, Montreal. Formally balanced, the repetition of triangular modules in the outer structure create a pattern of unity.

Woman and Bird Under the Moon (1944), Joan Miro, Spanish, Twentieth Century; oil on burlap. Collection, the Baltimore Museum of Art, Baltimore, Maryland, the May Collection.

Madonna and Child with Two Angels and Four Saints, Italian painting attributed to Niccolo di Pietro Gerini (active 1368 — C. 1415); tempera on panel, 21¾'' x 16''. Collection, the Baltimore Museum of Art, Saidie A. May Collection. The dignity and serenity of the formal balance of figures is emphasized by the architectural ornamentation framing the scene.

As you look at the works of the artist, designer, architect, craftsperson, try to think of them as something more than a painting, a colorful and attractive package for cereal, a stone and glass tower for offices, a ceramic bowl, a chair, an automobile. Examine these (and other) objects and note the way in which the artist uses line to create movement and pattern; how the designer uses color to give life and visual impact to an interior; the manner in which the architect relates shapes, forms and textures to produce balance and unity in his building.

These qualities of design are very important to the artist, the fashion designer, the automobile stylist, the product designer, the interior decorator, the architect, the commercial artist, the craftsperson. For as these creative persons develop ideas, prepare designs and translate them into final products with materials, they seek to achieve a sense of harmony and completeness in their creative work. They develop a feeling of balance and unity in their work by establishing varying degrees of contrast, pattern, emphasis, movement and rhythm within their designs. You may think of this as design organization or composition; the arrangement of lines, shapes, forms, colors, values and textures in a pleasing and attractive way.

The examples of art on these and the following pages were selected for two reasons: (1) To illustrate the broad realm of art; art beyond the museum and as a part of life today, and (2) To focus your attention on the different ways that artists achieve a sense of balance and unity in their work.

As you look at each individual work of art on these pages, what do you feel about it in terms of balance? Is it an example of formal balance? Informal balance? Radial balance? Why? Do all of the parts of a single design seem to fit together? Do you feel a spirit of unity in the design? If so, why? After you have studied these illustrations and made certain design judgments about them, look around you for other examples — in your community, displays in stores, products of industry, magazine and newspaper layouts and illustrations, outdoor art shows and museum exhibits, urban renewal areas and new houses. As your understanding of balance and unity (as well as other qualities of design) increase, your decision about things that you see, create and, in some instances, buy for personal use and enjoyment will have greater meaning to you as an individual.

"Rolled Up Voyage" (1963), Ferdinand Kriwet, graphic design, 23¾" in diameter. Collection, the Museum of Modern Art, New York. An illustration of radial balance. If you concentrate on this design, you should feel the powerful movement outward from the central point.

A neon symbol, this simple linear pattern is informal in balance by the necessary nature of its basic structure. Photograph by Al Porter.

Products of industry that are a part of our business world are also often representative of good design. Generally formal in balance, a sense of informality is projected through the pattern of keys and the lone wheel located on top to the right of center. These features contribute to the efficient function of the calculator. Victor Comptometer Corporation, Chicago, Illinois.

Peachtree Center Building, Atlanta, Georgia, a 27-story office building designed by Edwards and Portman, architects, echoes a strong feeling of unity through its repetitive pattern of rectangular windows, both vertically and horizontally. Bell and Stanton, Inc., public relations, New York City.

A dynamic treatment of an interior with contrasting chair forms, floor and wall textures and planting, successfully related to the graphics. Would you consider this formal or informal balance? Does this arrangement achieve a feeling of unity? Architectural Graphics Incorporated, Norfolk, Virginia.

The Furniture of Time (1939), Yves Tanguy, oil on canvas. The Museum of Modern Art, New York; collection James Thrall Soby, New Canaan, Connecticut. The rhythmic balance of individual shapes reaches deep into the picture plane; the delicate, angular lines contributing to unity in the design.

Indian Basket, Primitive Arts, the Baltimore Museum of Art, Maryland, Winslow bequest.

The art objects on these two pages are representative of radial balance, one in traditional Indian basketry, the other, an American household craft of the nineteenth century. The thrust of the design in each example is the radiating movement around a central point.

Sunflower Quilt (detail), ca. 1840, Rebecca Wilcox Birdsey, American. The
Baltimore Museum of Art, Maryland; gift of Miss Theora J. Bunnell.

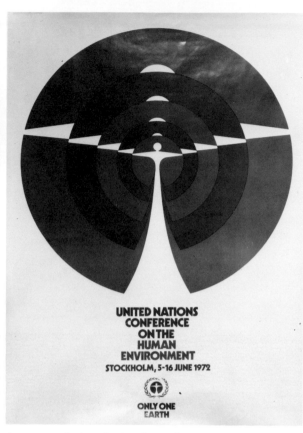

A poster. Is it a design based on formal or informal balance?

Edmund's windmill, an age-old device of mankind with a twentieth century look, has been designed as one possible answer to the energy crunch. For this piece of equipment to function at maximum efficiency, it must be balanced so that it can easily turn to capture the wind flow and convert it into electrical energy. Would you say that this design, silhouetted against the sky is a symbol of informal balance? Photo from PR Associates of Philadelphia, Inc. for Edmund Scientific Co., Barrington, New Jersey.

The appearance of products, such as this shiny row of new Suzukis, is often affected by your point of view. If you were standing directly in front of one of their motorcycles, the form that you would see would be basically formal balance. Whereas a side view, because of the function and nature of the machine, would appear to be quite informal in balance. Is there a part of the motorcycle that you would consider an example of radial balance? Photograph by Al Porter.

A massive, concrete bridge; an architectural innovation and an ancient Greek vase, how would you describe them in terms of balance?

A section of a concrete bridge, its sweeping arches and sturdy vertical supporting columns, giving assurance of safe crossing. Photograph by Al Porter.

La Verne College, California. A unique "super tent", composed of fiberglass yarns coated with teflon, this architectural structure houses a field house on the upper level; classrooms, recreational area and other spaces on the lower level. Note the relationship of the curved lines of the walkway to the design of the building, emphasizing the quality of unity. Photo by GTE Sylvania, Incorporated, which provided interior lighting for the structure, designed by Shaver Partnership, Salina, Kansas, architect.

Terra Cotta vase, Greek, Fifth Century B.C.; Panathenaic Amphora ca. 422 B.C., Two Boys Wrestling Before an Umpire, Attic (Niobid Painter). Collection, Baltimore Museum of Art, Maryland.

Throughout history the artist has interpreted the human form in many different ways. Here are four illustrations of contrasting styles of the artist. What is your reaction? Does each figure show a feeling of unity and balance? What kind of balance?

Figure of Warrior, bronze, height 12''; sculpture, African, Benin, Nigeria. Wurtzburger Collection of African Sculpture, The Baltimore Museum of Art.

Cooks Bay Figure, Oceanic Sculpture, New Guinea, Asmat Tribe; wood, 55½'' x 6½''. The Baltimore Museum of Art, Maryland, Gift of the Hecht Co.

Half-standing Figure, 1918, Jacques Lipchitz; bronze, 37'' high. The Baltimore Museum of Art, Maryland, Museum purchase, Fanny Thalheimer Bequest Fund.

Standing Venus, 1914, Pierre-Auguste Renoir (1841-1919), French, Nineteenth Century; Bronze sculpture, 23½''. Cone Collection, the Baltimore Museum of Art, Maryland.

Manzanita Hall, Arizona State University; Cartmell, Miller, Associates, architects; photograph by John Rogers of Dallas, Texas. An exciting architectural structure, the intriguing pattern of triangular shapes presents a spirit of unity as well as movement. Note, also, the repeat of the triangle motif as a structural element near the entrance.

A familiar phenomenon of the 1960's and 70's, graffiti on a once blank city wall, exemplifies confusion and disunity.

A university hall, a "decorated" wall and a clock of yesteryear, each of these in its own way plays a visual "tune" on your seeing capability. Each of these will motivate a different kind of design response. What are your reactions? Do you see organization, pattern, unity or disunity? How does balance relate?

Tall Case Clock, Baltimore, ca. 1773; Jacob Moler, maker. The Baltimore Museum of Art, Maryland; gift of the Friends of the American Wing.

What do these works of the artist/designer have in common?

Comp/set 500, a versatile, direct entry phototypesetter by Addressograph Multigraph Corporation, Ohio.

Atlantic Provinces Building at Expo 67, Montreal; the unusual, cantilevered roof itself represents a combination of physical balance with esthetic form.

The White Turban, Henri Matisse (1916), Oil on canvas. The Baltimore Museum of Art, Maryland, The Cone Collection.

SUMMARY

Design is everywhere in our natural and man-made environment. Some of the things that you see (automobiles, trees, buildings, flowers, magazines, clothes, shopping centers, bridges, home appliances, posters and many more) may be pleasing in design to you. Some you may not like; others may make no impression on you at all. Still others, such as, an abstract environmental sculpture or a non-objective painting, you may not understand. Yet they all will reflect, in varying degrees, the visual qualities of contrast, pattern, emphasis, movement, rhythm, balance and unity. Your awareness of these qualities of design will enable you to see more critically and to understand and appreciate at a higher level, the visual world in which you live.